Olivia Lauren's
GUIDE TO BECOMING AN ACTOR

Written and Illustrated by
Olivia Lauren & Melissa-Sue John, Ph.D.
Lauren Simone Publishing House

Library of Congress Cataloging-in-Publication Data

Lauren, Olivia and John, Melissa-Sue
Olivia Lauren's Guide to becoming an Actor/Olivia Lauren and Melissa-Sue John.
p. cm.
Illustration by Melissa-Sue John
Summary: A ten step guide for children interested in getting into the acting and modeling industry.
ISBN-13: 978-0-9979520-3-2 (paperback)
978-1-948071-36-9 (hardcover)
ISBN 10: 0997952032
Title I. Series.
1. Acting 2. Actor 3. Occupation 4. Jobs 5. Careers
2017900355

To Alkisha, Barbara, Eric, Frances, Linda, and Patricia

Hi, I am **Olivia Lauren!**

I am an **Actor.**

I have been in a number of well-known TV shows, films, **musicals, commercials,** and **music videos.**

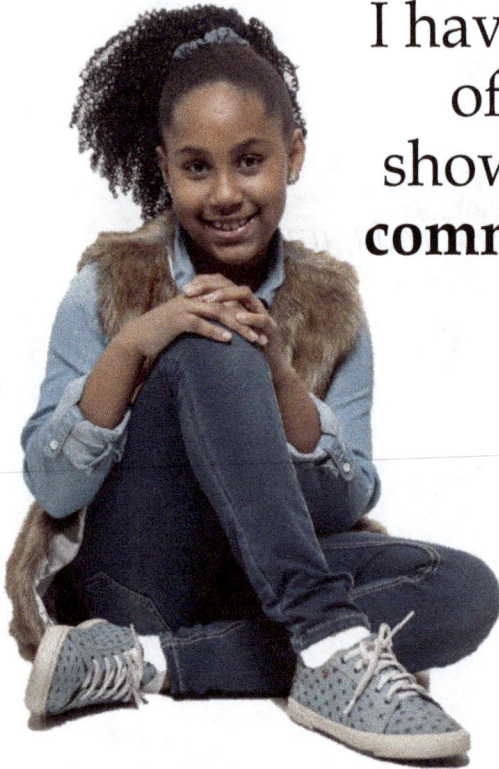

Photo Credit: @mikkajoe

Do you want to be an actor?

Before I even got to the stage or the TV screen, I had to go through a series of steps.

Here are 10 steps to becoming a child actor!

STEP 1: APPLY FOR A WORK PERMIT AND TRUST FUND

If you are a **minor,** you need a work permit.

In some states, child modeling, acting, or performing is regulated by labor laws.

Go online and search "Child performer permit" with the state you live. Follow the instructions and submit.

Photo Credit: @www.labor.ny.gov

Fifteen percent of your earnings is deposited into a trust fund and the remainder is mailed to you.

Go online or to your local Bank branch and set up a trust fund, also called a

COOGAN ACCOUNT

STEP 2: PROFESSIONAL PHOTOS

Snapshots are appropriate for babies, because they are constantly growing and changing.

But for older children, professional photos are recommended.

It shows that you are serious about being an actor and also that you are versatile and photogenic.

Photo Credit: @marykategutierrez

Find an experienced and affordable photographer.

Take headshots, three-quarter body, and full body portraits.

Keep it simple. No hats, glasses, or extra accessories. Smile with and without showing your teeth.

Photo Credit: @mikkajoe

Photo Credit: @marykategutierrez

STEP 3: FIND REPRESENTATION

Make a list of authentic **talent agencies** and **management companies** in the city nearest you.

Submit online OR by mail:

Professional photos
Age and Date of Birth
Height and Weight
Clothes and Shoe sizes
Contact Information
Area of Interest

Photo Credit: @laurensimonepubs

STEP 4: PREPARE TO AUDITION

Find a poem, **monologue,** song, or commercial script that you like.

Study the monologue until you can say it from memory and with confidence.

Photo Credit: @laurensimonepubs

Starting with a **slate**, create a **reel** by having your parent or a professional record your monologue.

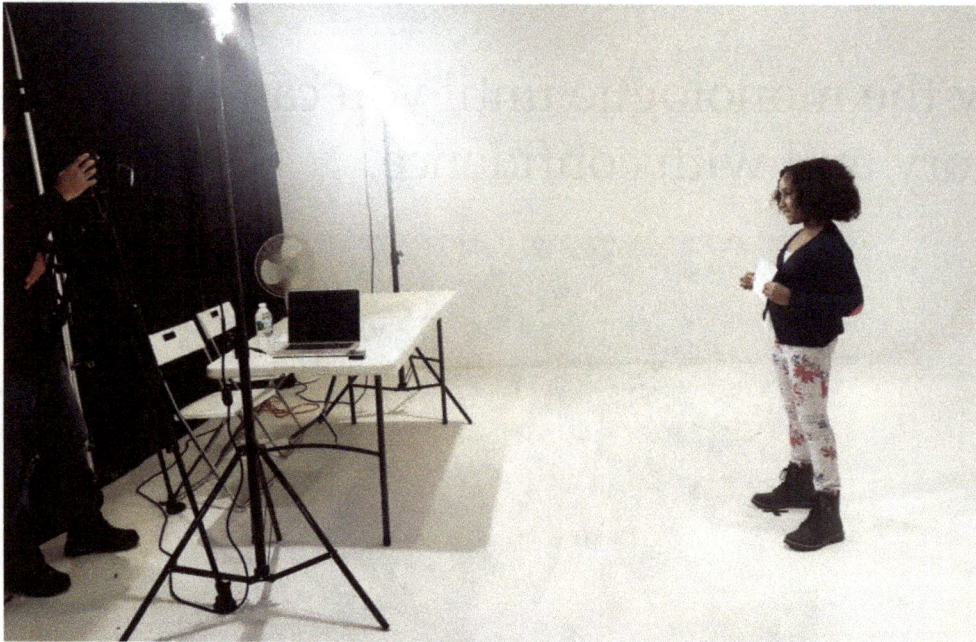

Photo Credit: @laurensimonepubs

STEP 5: PRACTICE YOUR ART

There are so many classes you can take to get training!

Acting for the camera

Improvisation

Performing arts

Voice lessons

Voice over

But you can learn as you go.

Photo Credit: @laurensimonepubs

STEP 6: GAIN EXPERIENCE

Gain training and acting experience through **student films** by signing up with nearby film schools.

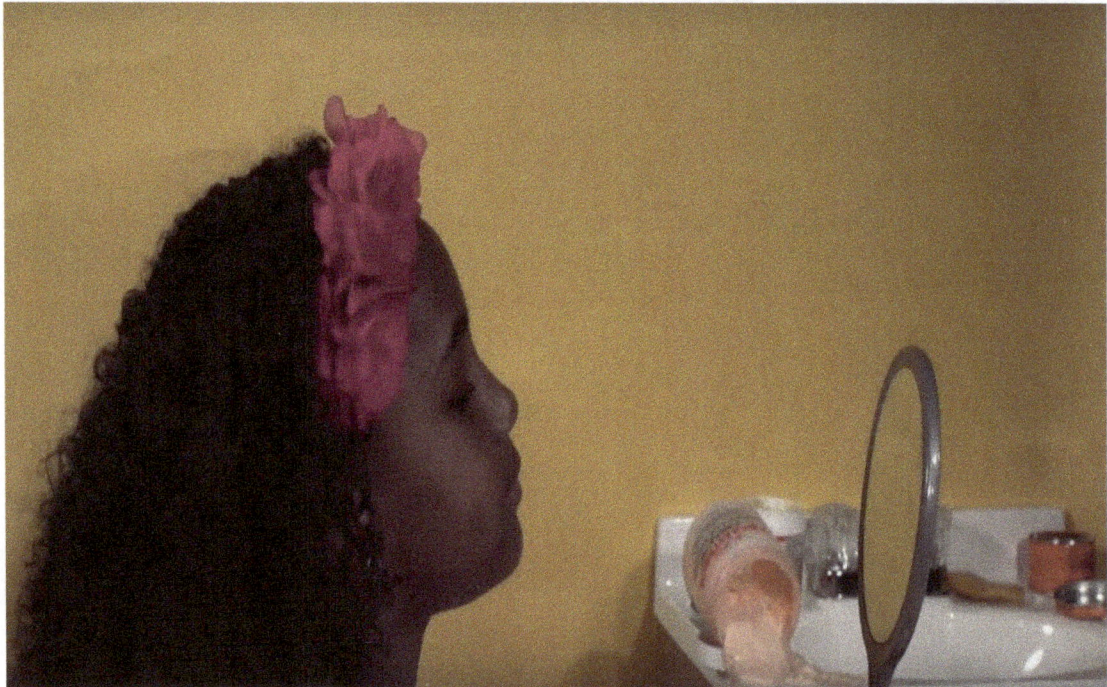

Photo Credit: @daequan

Sign up with **Casting Sites** for background acting and other gigs.

You will meet other actors, directors, and producers and learn the acting terminology: Action! Rolling! Reset.

Photo Credit: @laurensimonepubs

STEP 7: BE PATIENT...

Check your email, phone, and mailbox for communication from a manager, agent, or casting director regarding an **audition** or **direct booking**.

Photo Credit: @laurensimonepubs

Waiting is sometimes the hardest part. Be patient!

...AND BE YOU!

Keep in mind that the entertainment industry is very competitive.

There are many children trying out for the same roles and agencies.

Many children may be the same age, height, even have similar look or talent like you, but THERE IS ONLY ONE YOU!

Photo Credit: @mikkajoe

STEP 8: THE CALL BACK

When you least expect it, an agent, manager, or casting director will contact you for an audition, representation, or booking.

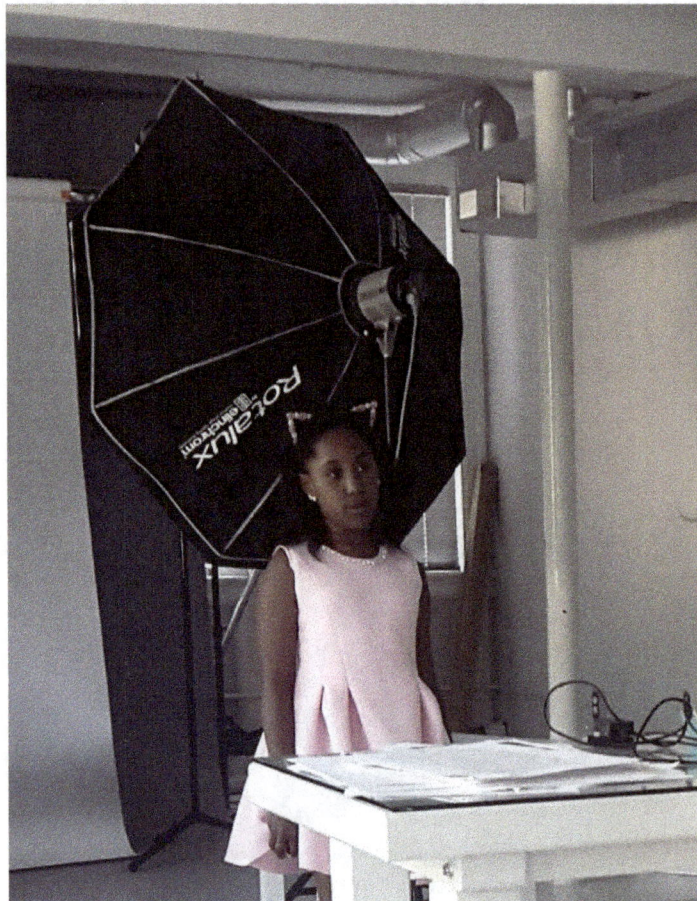

Photo Credit: @laurensimonepubs

STEP 9: BOOKED

Once you are booked, you will receive a **call sheet** telling you where and what time to show up on set.

Director: Ben Franklin bfranklin@gmail.com Producer: Natalia Perez nperez@gmail.com		Production: **Discovered in NY**	Date: June 4, 2016	
Weather Mostly Sunny Sunrise: 5:26am Sunset: 8:23pm		CALL TIME 10:30am 9:45AM Pre-Call for production and camera		
Location	Address	Parking	Notes	
1. East River Park	East River Park New York, NY	Street Parking outside park	Entry points on Delancey St. and Houston St.	
Scene Description	Cast	Pages	D/N	Location
Scene 1/2 Olivia and Justice at the park	1, 2, 3, BG	1/8	D	East River Park
Scene 2/2 Talent manager approaches Olivia and asks for her mom.	1, 2,3,4,5	2/8	D	East River Park
Number	Cast	Role	Call Time	Set Call
1	Olivia Lauren	Actor	10:30am	11:00am
2	Justice Lynn	Best friend	10:30am	11:00am
3	Alyssa Simone	Sister	10:30am	11:00am
4	Jennifer Brown	Talent manager	10:30am	11:00am
5	Linda Peters	Mother	10:30am	11:00am
BG	Kids	Kids playing in the park	10:30am	11:00am

Photo Credit: @laurensimonepubs

When you arrive, you will check in. Have your **photo ID** and **call number** ready.

You may be asked to sign a talent release and give copies of your permit and trust fund.

Photo Credit: @laurensimonepubs

You will meet with **wardrobe** and **hair and make up** crew.

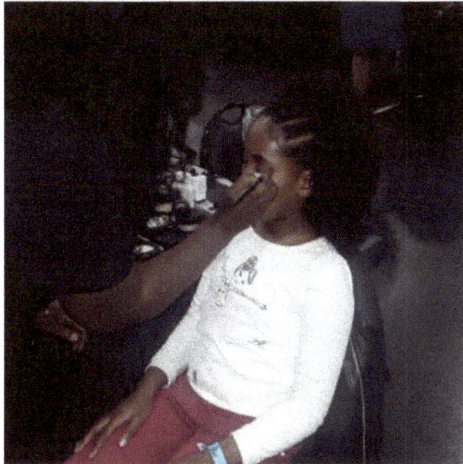

Finally, you get to go on **set** to start filming.

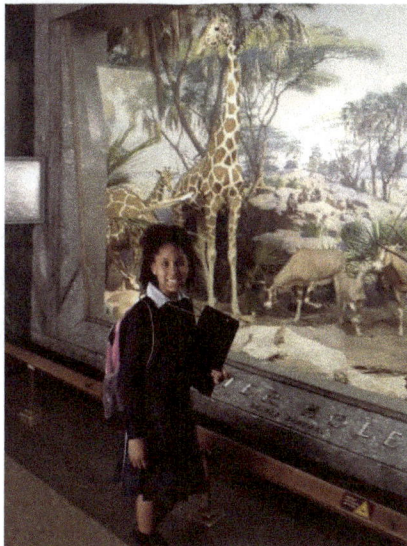

Photo Credit: @laurensimonepubs

STEP 10: GET CREDIT

As a **principal actor**, you may see your name in the credits at the beginning or the end of the production.

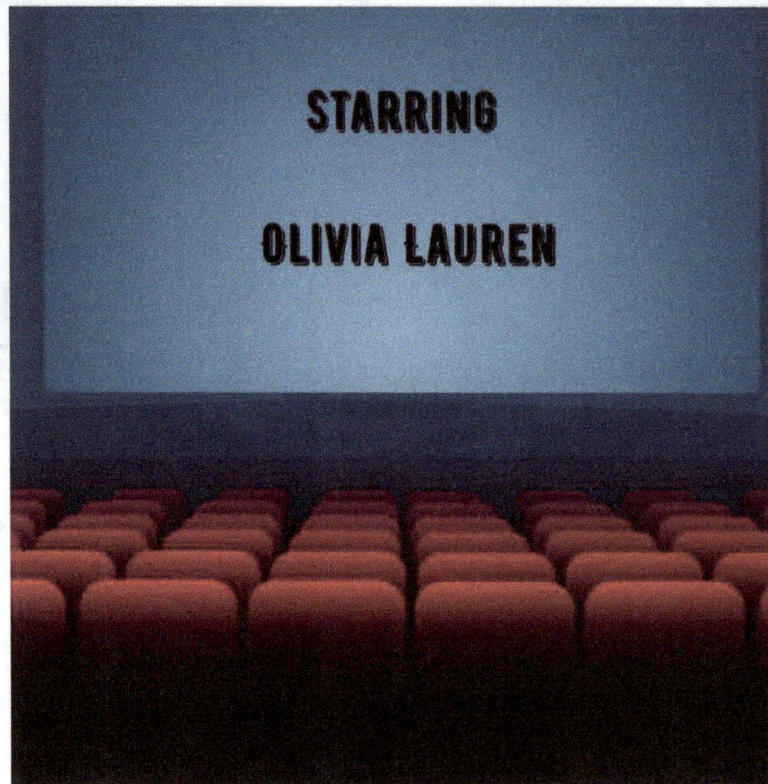

STARRING

OLIVIA LAUREN

Photo Credit: @laurensimonepubs

BE PROUD OF YOURSELF

No matter what **role** you play, you should always feel proud of yourself!

Photo Credit: @uponsugarhill

IMDb

If you had a principal or supporting role, you will get credit as a **cast member.**

You can search for your credits on the **internet movie database** (IMDb).

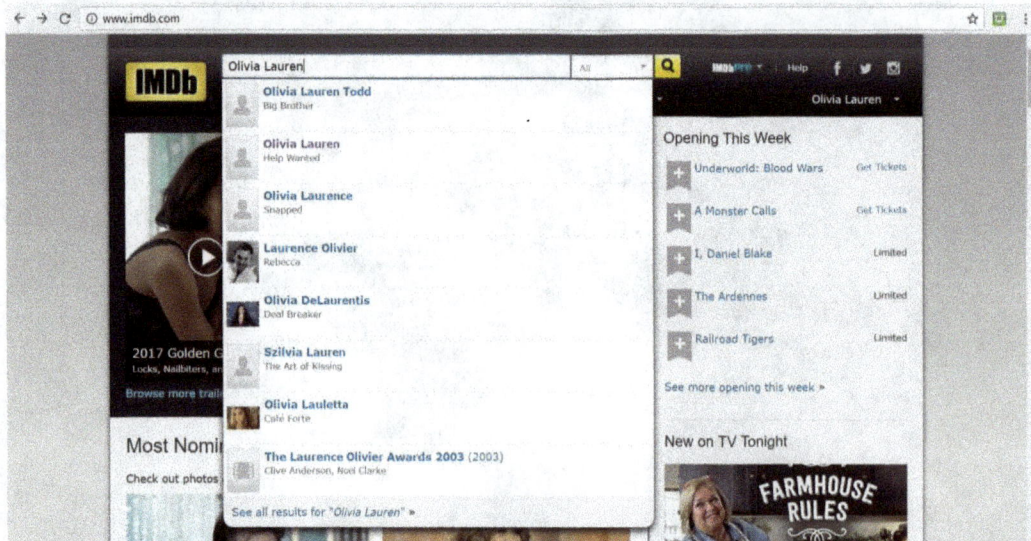

Photo Credit: www.imdb.com

CONGRATULATIONS

This is the moment you have been waiting for!

It's official you are an actor, just like me.

Follow me on Instagram **@olivialaurenj**

GLOSSARY

Actor: one who performs for the entertainment of others.

Agent: a person who submits talent for jobs.

Areas of interest: print, commercial, voiceover, theater, television, or film.

Audition: when a person tries out for an acting job.

Background actor: a nonspeaking actor in a production.

Booked: when an entertainer gets a job.

Call back: a second audition.

Call number: the number on the call sheet next to your name.

Call sheet: a document that has the name, contact information, report location, and report times for all the cast and crew members.

Casting director: a person who finds actors for the characters in a movie, TV show, or play.

Cast member: a principal actor in a production.

Crew member: a person involved in filming and producing the film.

Commercial: television or radio advertisement.

Direct booking: getting a job based on your photo without having auditioned.

Hair and makeup crew: a team of professional hair stylists and makeup experts that provide hair styling and makeup for actors.

Headshot: a professional photograph, usually a close shot of your face and chest, used to cast acting jobs.

Improvisation: acting on the spot without preparation.

Internet movie database (IMDb): an online source that lists information on cast, production, crew, characters, plot, and reviews.

Management company: a company that provides a manager for the talent and works with many agencies to help develop the talent's career.

Minor: a person under the age of 18 years old.

Monologue: a written text like a poem, commercial, or movie script.

Music video: television recording to a popular song.

Musical: performance in a theater that includes speaking, singing, and dancing.

Photo ID: identification with your photograph such as a passport or school or government ID

Principal actor: an actor with a speaking role in a production.

Reel: a taped recording.

Role: the character played in a production.

Set: the place in which the TV show, film, or play is being produced.

Script: the written text of a TV show, movie, play, or other broadcast.

Slate: a paper or movie board used to identify the actor (name, age, part auditioning for, contact information) or production before filming.

Student film: a film directed and produced by college students who often need volunteers to perform in their class projects.

Talent agency: a company that provides the talent an agent to book them jobs.

Trust fund: a savings account for your future.

Voice over: speaking role without being on camera, usually the voice of a cartoon or the narrator of a commercial.

Wardrobe crew: members of the film crew who decide what each character should wear on set.

Work permit: informs the production company hiring you that you have permission to work in that state.

OLIVIA LAUREN BOOK SERIES

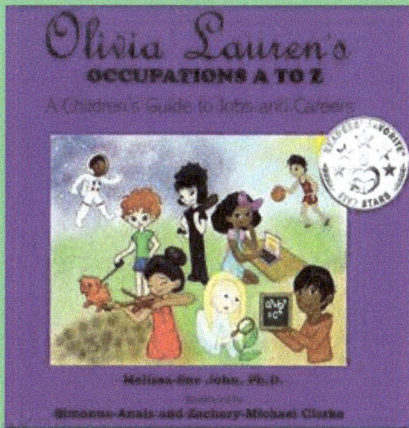

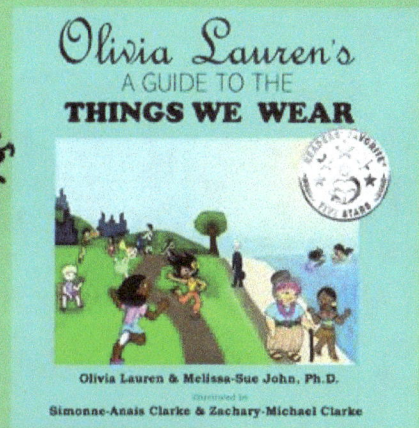

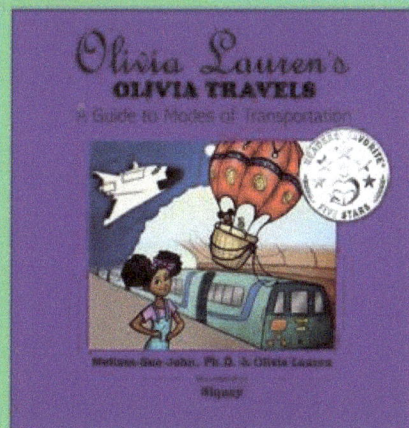

Lauren Simone
PUBLISHING HOUSE

Olivia Lauren's OCCUPATIONS A TO Z
A Children's Guide to Jobs and Careers
Melissa-Sue John, Ph.D.
Illustrated by Simonne-Anais and Zachary-Michael Clarke

Olivia Lauren's A GUIDE TO THE THINGS WE WEAR
Olivia Lauren & Melissa-Sue John, Ph.D.
Illustrated by Simonne-Anais Clarke & Zachary-Michael Clarke

Olivia Lauren's OLIVIA CONNECTS
A Guide to Modes of Communication
Melissa-Sue John, Ph.D. & Alyssa Simone
Illustrated by Lionel Emabat

Olivia Lauren's OLIVIA TRAVELS
A Guide to Modes of Transportation
Melissa-Sue John, Ph.D. & Olivia Lauren
Illustrated by Sigany

www.ingramcontent.com/pod-product-compliance
Lightning Source LLC
Chambersburg PA
CBHW050639150426
42813CB00054B/1118